MW01154360

This book
belongs to

_____

_____

Noah's Fascinating
World of STEAM Experiments

Noah's Fascinating World of STEAM Experiments

CHEMICAL REACTIONS

Sarah Habibi, PhD
@SarahAHabibi

mango
PUBLISHING GROUP

CORAL GABLES

Copyright © 2023 by Sarah Habibi, PhD.
Published by Mango Publishing, a division of Mango Publishing Group, Inc.

Cover Design: Elina Diaz
Cover Photo/illustration: Sarah Habibi, PhD, and adobe.stock.com
Interior illustrations: Anatomii Studio
Layout & Design: Elina Diaz

Mango is an active supporter of authors' rights to free speech and artistic expression in their books. The purpose of copyright is to encourage authors to produce exceptional works that enrich our culture and our open society.

Uploading or distributing photos, scans or any content from this book without prior permission is theft of the author's intellectual property. Please honor the author's work as you would your own. Thank you in advance for respecting our author's rights.

For permission requests, please contact the publisher at:
Mango Publishing Group
2850 S Douglas Road, 2nd Floor
Coral Gables, FL 33134 USA
info@mango.bz

For special orders, quantity sales, course adoptions and corporate sales, please email the publisher at sales@mango. bz. For trade and wholesale sales, please contact Ingram Publisher Services at customer.service@ingramcontent.com or +1.800.509.4887.

Noah's Fascinating World of STEAM Experiments: Chemical Reactions

Library of Congress Cataloging-in-Publication number: 2023935071
ISBN: (paperback) 978-1-68481-175-5, (hard cover) 978-1-68481-321-6 (ebook) 978-1-68481-176-2
BISAC category code JNF051070, JUVENILE NONFICTION / Science & Nature / Chemistry

"Creativity is intelligence having fun."
—Albert Einstein

Table of Contents

Welcome!

Hey, scientists! My name is Noah, and I love science! It's time for you to put your lab coats on and join me on this journey as we explore chemical reactions! Be sure to write your name in this book, as you make your mark as a scientist in training.

This book is going to take you on an exciting journey as you explore STEAM (Science, Technology, Engineering, Art, and Mathematics) experiments in your home! All ten of these experiments will teach you about chemical reactions. What is a chemical reaction, you might ask? Keep reading and you will learn all about them!

As you work through each experiment, you will be encouraged to follow along as a junior scientist and take part in what we call the scientific process. This process includes guessing what will happen in each experiment, drawing what you see when things are mixed together, and changing parts of the experiment to make it work better.

In the end, this book will be filled with all of your writings and drawings and will resemble a real scientist's lab notebook. That's right, you are creating your very first lab notebook! This will be a book you can keep and look back on in many years to come.

My mom is a scientist and still has her lab notebooks from over ten years ago!

Get ready, because the experiments we are about to explore are BUBBLY, COLOURFUL, BIG, and MIND-BLOWING! Let's get started!

All About Chemical Reactions

Chemical reactions are not only done in science laboratories; they also take place all around us, all day, every day. In fact, there are chemical reactions happening all throughout your body as you read this book! Chemical reactions are required for life, and scientists can explore and learn about them by doing experiments.

One thing all the experiments in this book have in common is that they are chemical reactions. A **chemical reaction** happens when one or more substances (**reactants**) are transformed into something new (**products**).

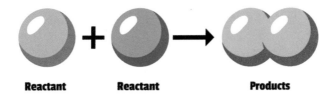

Reactant   Reactant   Products

Standard equation for a chemical reaction.

We can see a chemical reaction happen when bubbles form, colour changes, heat or cold is given off, or gas is formed.

What makes chemical reactions special and unique is that sometimes, when a substance is changed into something new, it can't be changed back into what it was in the beginning. An experiment with a substance that cannot be changed back into what it was before is called an **irreversible chemical reaction**. Most of the experiments we will do in this book will be irreversible. So what you observe at the end of the experiment will be the final and only product. While you won't be able to reverse the results of an experiment, if the product of your experiment is different from what it should be, you may need to try again. Follow the step-by-step instructions more carefully, or change a step to get different results.

An example of an irreversible chemical reaction would be burning a leaf. Once the leaf catches on fire and burns, it transforms into ash, and it can't change back into a pretty leaf again. An example of a reversible chemical reaction would be cleaning the rust off of an old copper penny—an experiment we will look at later in this book!

In the chapters to follow, you will carry out ten STEAM experiments that are all examples of chemical reactions.

Elephant Toothpaste

The star of the first chemical reaction is **hydrogen peroxide**.

 My mom uses hydrogen peroxide on my skin when I get cuts and scrapes on my knees while practicing my new skateboarding skills! She says it helps to clean the cut by killing bacteria.

Hydrogen peroxide is kept in a dark brown bottle because, when the light touches it, it goes through a chemical reaction and starts to transform into water and **oxygen gas** (like the air we breathe).

We call this experiment elephant toothpaste because it is bubbly, explosive, and big enough to be toothpaste for a huge elephant! But it's just pretend toothpaste and not real toothpaste. Unfortunately, we can't use this to clean a real elephant's teeth, or human teeth. We are simply doing this experiment to learn.

Junior scientists, let's explore our own chemical reaction and make some elephant toothpaste!

Activity 1: Hypothesis

One of the first steps a scientist takes when preparing to conduct an experiment is to make an educated guess on what will happen at the end of the science experiment. This guess is called a **hypothesis**! In this experiment, we are going to mix dish soap with hydrogen peroxide. Write down what you think will happen when we mix everything together. What will it look like? Your prediction is your hypothesis.

Use this space to write down your hypothesis.

Experiment Time!

Let's begin! Start by gathering all of your materials for the experiment. Here is the list! Remember, none of these materials should be eaten!

Materials

- 500 ml empty water bottle (or similar)
- Bottle of 3 percent hydrogen peroxide
- Dish soap
- 1 packet of instant yeast (8 grams)
- Warm water
- Food colouring of choice
- ½-cup measuring cup
- 1-tablespoon measuring spoon
- ½-tablespoon measuring spoon
- Funnel
- Small cup
- Spoon
- Paper towel
- Large dish
- Timer

Now we have all of our materials ready.

Methods

During the methods section of each experiment, you will follow step-by-step **instructions** on how to complete the experiment. As a junior scientist, you need to follow these instructions carefully and complete each step exactly as it is written. This will help make sure that you get the expected results at the end of the experiment. The methods section of each experiment will be split into two parts to allow you to watch the experiment and make observations along the way.

Pouring hydrogen peroxide into water bottle using a funnel.

Adding dish soap to water bottle.

Adding food colouring to water bottle.

Let's dive into part one of the methods for this experiment!

1. Begin by taking your ½-cup measuring cup and pouring the hydrogen peroxide into it. Using the funnel, carefully pour the ½ cup of hydrogen peroxide into your empty water bottle.

2. Next, measure ½ tablespoon of dish soap using the ½-tablespoon measuring spoon. Add the measured dish soap into the same water bottle.

3. Finally, add five to ten drops of your favourite colour of food colouring into the water bottle.

Watch how to make elephant toothpaste here!

Activity 2: Observations

Before we continue, embrace your artist skills and draw what the water bottle looks like after you added the hydrogen peroxide, dish soap, and food colouring! This is something scientists do all the time. They draw and write out what they see happening in a science experiment every step of the way. This is called **documentation**.

Use the space below to draw what you see!

Experiment Time!

Now that we've gone through the first few phases of the experiment, let's continue to the best part!

Methods Continued

Mixing instant yeast in water for one minute.

Pouring yeast mixture into water bottle using a funnel.

Elephant toothpaste forming.

1. In a small cup, mix together a packet of instant yeast with 3 tablespoons of warm water. Mix with a spoon for one minute. Use a timer to keep track of your one minute of mixing.

2. Using a funnel, quickly add the yeast and water mixture to the water bottle, remove the funnel right away, and step back. Watch the reaction take place.

Remember scientists, never eat anything while doing science experiments. Do not snack on or eat any of the materials used during this experiment, either. It will taste pretty gross anyways!

Activity 3: Results

WOW! Wasn't that explosive?

After a scientist finishes a science experiment, they write down and draw what they saw happen. This is called **collecting the results**.

This step is important because it gives scientists an opportunity to look back on experiments they did in the past. It helps scientists remember the results exactly as they happened.

This gives you the opportunity to look back on the experiments you do in this book and remember all of the explosive results you saw!

Draw what you saw happen when the yeast mixture was added to the bottle.

What's the Science?

In this experiment, we made elephant toothpaste by carrying out a chemical reaction. Remember, the star of this chemical reaction is hydrogen peroxide.

When hydrogen peroxide is exposed to light, it slowly breaks down into water and oxygen gas. This process is very slow, BUT you can add something to make the reaction go faster!

Substances that help speed up reactions are called **catalysts**. A catalyst provides a special environment to help transform reactants into products quickly.

In this reaction, the catalyst is yeast! Yeast contains a special chemical called catalase. Catalase acts to help break down the hydrogen peroxide into water and oxygen gas quicker. This is why you didn't see the elephant toothpaste bubble up and shoot out of the bottle until the yeast was added.

The other star ingredient in this experiment is the dish soap. The oxygen gas formed in this chemical reaction takes the form of tiny bubbles. Those bubbles want to escape into the air. Instead, they are first trapped in the dish soap, causing even bigger bubbles to escape out the top of the bottle. There are so many of these bubbles, they look like a large foam. That is what we call elephant toothpaste!

Let's Try Again

Oh no! Something went wrong. Did the experiment not go as planned? Why didn't the foam shoot out of the top of the water bottle?

Let's take a look.

Don't worry, junior scientists, this happens all the time! It is very common for experiments not to work out the first time around.

There are a few points in this experiment where something could have gone wrong. The first place is when dish soap was added to the water bottle. Perhaps you didn't add enough?

The second place where something could have gone wrong is when you prepared the yeast mixture and added it to the water bottle. Perhaps the yeast wasn't fully mixed, or the water was too hot or too cold?

Here are some suggestions for how you can modify, or change, the experiment to get better and more explosive results!

Modified Methods

1. Add 1 tablespoon of dish soap instead of ½ tablespoon.

2. Add warm water to the yeast, mix for three minutes, and immediately add to the water bottle.

3. Use a new packet of instant yeast.

Activity 4: Your Turn!

When an experiment doesn't go as planned, scientists will modify a part of the experiment, try again, and observe to see if they get a different result. Scientists make modifications and redo experiments until they get the results they are looking for. This process is called **trial and error**.

Use the suggestions to plan out a new experiment. First, write out your hypothesis for the modified experiment. (What do you think will happen differently?) Next, write out the modified methods you followed. And finally, complete the new experiment by following your modified methods and observe the results you get.

 It's your time to shine, junior scientists! Use the following sections to write out how you changed your experiment. Be sure to share your results!

Trial 1

The first modification involves adding 1 tablespoon of dish soap instead of ½ tablespoon.

Hypothesis

_____

_____

_____

_____

_____

Modified Methods

_____

_____

_____

_____

_____

_____

_____

_____

_____

_____

_____

Trial 2

The second modification involves adding warm water to the yeast, mixing for three minutes, and immediately adding it to the water bottle.

Hypothesis

_____

_____

_____

_____

_____

_____

Modified Methods

Results

Trial 3

The third modification involves using a new packet of instant yeast.

Hypothesis

_____

_____

_____

_____

_____

Modified Methods

_____

_____

_____

_____

_____

Results

Well done! You are on your way to becoming a great scientist!

Loony Lava Lamp

What's bubbly, colourful, and mesmerizing to watch?

A LAVA LAMP!

The star in this chemical reaction is an Alka-Seltzer tablet! Alka-Seltzer tablets contain a compound called **sodium bicarbonate**. When the tablets are placed in water, they break down and produce **carbon dioxide gas**.

This carbon dioxide gas is going to be key for making our lava lamp POP!

In this experiment, we use water and oil as the base of the lava lamp. Did you know a traditional lava lamp doesn't use oil at all? Instead, wax is used in a traditional lava lamp. But don't worry, scientists, whether we use oil or wax, we are still experimenting with making a lava lamp.

The man who invented traditional lava lamps in the 1960s first got the idea while eating breakfast at a restaurant. The man saw this cup of water full of wax by the chef cooking his eggs. The chef explained to him that a candle put under the cup heated up the wax in the water, and when the wax melted and floated to the top of the cup, that meant the eggs he was cooking were perfectly cooked. The chef used this as a timer for cooking eggs. This egg timer is what inspired the man to design what we now know as a lava lamp! Talk about an EGG-celent idea!

Let's get started!

Activity 1: Hypothesis

In this experiment, you will add water and oil into a water bottle. Touch the water and then touch the oil. Do you notice that water feels wet, and the oil feels slippery? What do you think will happen when we mix the water and oil together?

Use this space to write down your hypothesis.

_____

_____

_____

_____

_____

_____

_____

_____

_____

_____

_____

_____

Experiment Time!

Let's start by gathering all of the materials we will need for the experiment.

Here is the list! Remember, none of these materials should be eaten.

Materials

- 500 ml empty water bottle (or similar)
- Water
- Bottle of vegetable oil
- 1 pack of Alka-Seltzer tablets (more can be used)
- Food colouring of choice
- Cup for mixing
- Measuring cups (1-cup and ½-cup)
- Spoon
- Funnel

Now that we have all of our materials, let's get ready to experiment!

Methods

1. Begin by taking your ½-cup measuring cup and measuring ½ cup of water. Then, pour it into a cup.

2. Add ten drops of your favourite food colouring to the cup of water. Mix with a spoon.

3. Using a funnel, pour the coloured water into the water bottle.

4. Slowly add 2 cups of vegetable oil to the water bottle containing the coloured water.

Watch how to make a lava lamp here!

Measuring water using a
½-cup measuring cup.

Adding food
colouring to water.

Pouring coloured water into the
water bottle using a funnel.

Pouring vegetable oil into the
water bottle using a funnel.

Water bottle containing
coloured water and
vegetable oil.

Activity 2: Observations

Before we continue, remember we must tap into our inner artist and draw what the water bottle looks like after you added the vegetable oil and water. Do you notice anything special about where the water and oil are located within the bottle?

Use the space below to draw what you see! Get creative and add colours to make your observation POP!

Experiment Time!

It's time for the most exciting part of the experiment!

Methods Continued

Alka-Seltzer tablet broken in half.

Adding Alka-Seltzer tablet to the water bottle.

Lava lamp.

1. Open the pack of Alka-Seltzer tablets and take out one tablet. Break the tablet in half.

2. Add the tablet to the water bottle (breaking it up in case it doesn't fit whole) and watch the reaction take place!

Hey junior scientist! Did you know you can keep the reaction going and going? All you need to do is keep adding a new Alka-Seltzer tablet once the bubbles stop. Try it!

Activity 3: Results

How mesmerizing is that lava lamp?

It's that time again! Put your artist skills to the test and draw out the results of this experiment. You can also write out what you saw happen.

Draw what you saw happen in the water bottle after you added the Alka-Seltzer tablets.

What's the Science?

In this experiment, we made a lava lamp by carrying out a chemical reaction. In the first half of the experiment, you added coloured water and vegetable oil to the water bottle. Oil is less dense than water. That means oil is lighter and water is heavier. Because of this, the water sinks to the bottom of the bottle, and the oil floats on top.

Now let's talk about the second half of the experiment. Remember, the star of this chemical reaction is an Alka-Seltzer tablet.

One of the main components in Alka-Seltzer tablets is sodium bicarbonate. When the Alka-Seltzer tablets are placed in water, the sodium bicarbonate breaks down and carbon dioxide gas is released.

The Alka-Seltzer tablet sinks to the bottom of the water bottle when it is added because it is heavy. Remember, the bottom of the water bottle is filled with water. The water creates an environment where the tablet can be broken down into carbon dioxide gas.

The carbon dioxide gas gets trapped in tiny water droplets and wants to escape into the air. Since the carbon dioxide gas makes the water droplets less dense (lighter) than oil, the droplets can float up to the top of the water bottle. Once the droplets reach the top of the oil, they pop and release the carbon dioxide gas into the air.

After the water droplets pop at the top of the bottle, they become more dense (heavier) than oil again and float back down to the bottom of the bottle, where they grab more carbon dioxide gas and repeat the process. The process of water droplets floating up to the top of the bottle and back down to the bottom is what gives the appearance of a lava lamp.

Talk about a science experiment that really POPS!

Let's Try Again

Oh no! Something went wrong. Did the experiment not go as planned? Why didn't many bubbles form?

Let's take a look.

 I love this experiment because it works almost every time! But that doesn't mean we can't make it even better! Check out this tip to make your lava lamp POP even more!

This tip is all about surface area. **Surface area** is the total measure of the outside surface of an object. The surface area of the Alka-Seltzer tablet is the surface on the outside of the tablet (the top, bottom, and side).

The bigger the surface area, the more space there is for water to react with the tablet and for carbon dioxide gas to form. That means that, if we break the tablet up into smaller pieces, we create more surface area for the reaction to take place. This makes more carbon dioxide and more bubbles!

Give the following a try!

Modified Methods

1. Break an Alka-Seltzer tablet into four pieces. Place the four pieces into the water bottle.

2. Get two Alka-Seltzer tablets. Break them both into four pieces. Add all eight pieces into the water bottle.

Activity 4: Your Turn!

Use the suggestions to plan a new experiment. Complete the new experiment and observe the results you get.

Trial 1

The first modification involves breaking an Alka-Seltzer tablet into four pieces and adding it to the water bottle.

Hypothesis

_____

_____

_____

_____

_____

Modified Methods

_____

_____

_____

_____

_____

Results

_____

_____

_____

_____

_____

_____

Trial 2

The second modification involves breaking two Alka-Seltzer tablet into four pieces each (eight pieces total) and adding them to the water bottle.

Hypothesis

_____

_____

_____

_____

_____

_____

Modified Methods

Results

**Well done!
On to the next
experiment we go!**

Slimy Slime

 Do you like getting your hands dirty? I sure do! And so does my mom! This is one of my favourite science experiments to get my hands dirty in!

Slime has been in the spotlight for quite a few years now. But did you know that a chemical reaction is the reason why slime is squishy, stretchy, and fun to play with?

One of the star ingredients in this chemical reaction is polyvinyl alcohol (also known as PVA), which is found in white glue. The other star ingredient in this reaction is contact lens solution. Contact lens solution is a salt water solution used to clean contact lenses and keep them hydrated.

The best part about this experiment is that you can make this super slimy slime using a few key ingredients that can all be found in your home!

Are you ready to get your hands dirty? Let's go!

Activity 1: Hypothesis

In this experiment, you will be adding three main ingredients together: glue, baking soda, and contact lens solution. The slime begins to form when the final ingredient, contact solution, is added to the mixture. What do you think happens when a little contact solution is slowly added to the glue?

Use this space to write down your hypothesis.

Experiment Time!

As always, we are going to start by getting all of our ingredients together in one place. Ready, set, GO! Here is the list!

Materials

- Clear or white liquid glue (also known as school glue or PVA glue)
- Baking soda
- Contact lens solution
- Mixing bowl
- Glitter (optional)
- Spoon
- Measuring cup (1 cup)
- 1-tablespoon measuring spoon
- ½-teaspoon measuring spoon
- Paper towel

Now that all of the materials are ready, it's time to experiment!

Methods

1. Measure 1 cup of liquid glue and add it to your mixing bowl.
2. Measure 1 teaspoon of baking soda and add it to the same mixing bowl.
3. Mix together using a spoon.
4. Optional step: Measure ½ teaspoon of the glitter of your choice and add it to the same mixing bowl. Mix together using the spoon.

Watch how to make slime here!

Adding clear liquid glue to the mixing bowl using a 1-cup measuring cup.

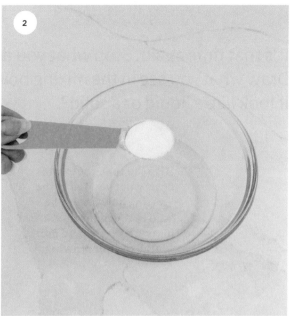

Adding baking soda to a bowl of clear glue using a 1-teaspoon measuring spoon.

Mixing baking soda into clear glue.

Mixing glitter into clear glue.

Activity 2: Observations

It's that time again! Stop what you are doing and put your artist hat on. Draw what you see in the mixing bowl. What does the glue look like? Does it look like a liquid or a solid?

Use the space below to draw what you see in the mixing bowl! Don't be afraid to touch the mixture. This will help you add more detail to your drawing.

Experiment Time!

Are you ready to get messy? It's time to make some SLIMY SLIME!

Methods Continued

Adding a tablespoon of contact lens solution to the glue mixture.

Mixing contact lens solution into glue mixture with a spoon.

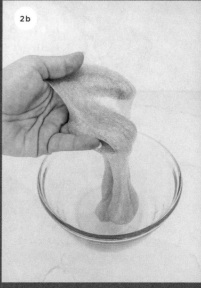
Mixing formed slime in hands.

1. Measure 1 tablespoon of contact lens solution. Add it to the mixing bowl. Begin mixing the glue with a spoon.

2. Measure another tablespoon of contact solution. Add it to the mixing bowl. This time, start mixing everything in the bowl together with your hands.

Hey, junior scientist! What do you notice about the temperature of the glue mixture? Does it feel cold? That's because this chemical reaction is an endothermic reaction. You will learn more about these types of chemical reactions in the "What's the Science?" part of this experiment.

Activity 3: Results

How satisfying is it to squish the slime between your fingers?

Let's take a moment to clean our hands so that we can once again put our artist skills to the test!

 Draw a picture of the slime you created in the space below. Try moulding the slime into different shapes and drawing those shapes. What happens when you leave the slime shape on the table for a few minutes? Does it change into a new shape? Draw what you see happening over time!

What's the Science?

In this experiment, slime is created by the chemical reaction between two main ingredients. The two ingredients are **polyvinyl alcohol** (PVA), which is found in the glue you used, and **borate ions**. Borate ions, however, were not added directly to the glue. Instead, the two other ingredients, baking soda and contact lens solution, reacted to make borate ions when they were mixed together.

Baking soda contains **sodium bicarbonate**. Contact solution contains **boric acid** and **sodium borate**. When sodium bicarbonate, boric acid, and sodium borate are mixed together, they undergo a chemical reaction that produces borate ions. These borate ions act as an **activator** by causing the glue to become thick through a process called **cross-linking**.

There are many different slime activators that you can choose from. Other activators include liquid starch, borax powder, and saline solution (salt water). The one thing that all these activators have in common is that they are all part of the boron element family, group 13 (formerly III) on the periodic table.

Before we dive into learning more about cross-linking, we first need to learn about polymers! A **polymer** is a long chain of molecules. You can imagine this as a string with a bunch of beads on it, all repeating after one another to make a bracelet. The glue used to make the slime is made up of long polymers of polyvinyl acetate molecules. These long polymers slide past each other freely, which is what makes glue flow like a liquid.

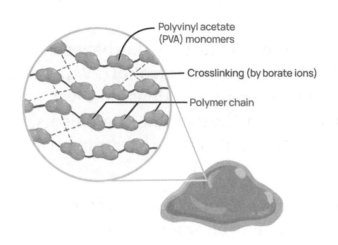

- Polyvinyl acetate (PVA) monomers
- Crosslinking (by borate ions)
- Polymer chain

Cross-linking of PVA molecules in polymer chain.

Now back to the slime! Cross-linking happens when the slime activator changes the position of the polymer molecules in the glue. You can think of this as making the molecules in the glue nice and tightly packed together. This packing of molecules changes the thickness of the glue, and the long polymers are no longer able to slide past each other freely. As a result, the glue flows less and acts more like a solid.

So, is slime a solid or a liquid? The answer is BOTH! Substances that act as both a solid and a liquid are known as **non-Newtonian fluids**. A non-Newtonian fluid like slime can be picked up like a ball, but can also squish between your fingers like water. You may notice that you can form the slime into shapes, but after you leave those shapes on a flat surface for a few minutes, they flow down into a "puddle" of slime again.

Finally, let's learn about why your slime felt cold to the touch when you first mixed all of the ingredients together. The chemical reaction that took place to make the slime is known as an **endothermic reaction**. Endothermic reactions absorb heat from their surroundings, causing them to feel cold to the touch. The opposite of this type of chemical reaction is an **exothermic reaction**. Exothermic reactions release heat into their surroundings, causing them to feel warm or hot to the touch.

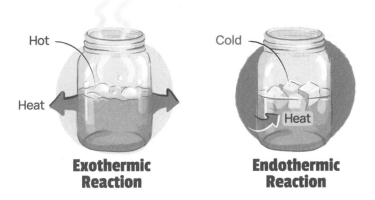

Exothermic Reaction **Endothermic Reaction**

Wow, this experiment was filled with messy, slimy fun and A LOT of science! You are learning so much, junior scientists!

Let's Try Again

Oh no! Did the slime not come out as planned? Or, maybe you want to change it up to be more or less slimy!

Let's dive into some places where you can modify this experiment.

I love slime that is super gooey and not so hard. My mom and I love getting our hands dirty as we stretch and play with the slime. Let's take a look at how we can make our slime more gooey!

Modified Methods

1. Before adding the contact lens solution, add 2 tablespoons of water to the glue mixture.

2. Add 3 tablespoons of contact solution instead of 2.

Activity 4: Your Turn!

Use the suggestions to plan a new experiment. Complete the new experiment and observe the results you get.

Trial 1

The first modification involves adding 2 tablespoons of water to the glue mixture before adding the contact lens solution.

Hypothesis

_____

_____

_____

_____

_____

Modified Methods

_____

_____

_____

_____

_____

_____

_____

_____

_____

_____

_____

Trial 2

The second modification involves adding 3 tablespoons of contact lens solution to the glue mixture.

Hypothesis

_____

_____

_____

_____

_____

_____

_____

Modified Methods

_____

_____

_____

_____

_____

_____

Results

_____

_____

_____

_____

_____

_____

Awesome work!
Time to wash your
hands and move
on to the next
experiment!

Foaming Shapes

Do you remember making elephant toothpaste at the beginning of this book? Well, this next experiment is also super bubbly and fun to watch! The best part is, you can make the experiment into anything you want! Seriously, let me show you!

In this experiment, you have the opportunity to mould a substance into any shape you want. Maybe you make a snowman, or a star, or a dog. You have the freedom here to make whatever you want! This shape that you mould will be the base of the chemical reaction.

The star ingredients of this chemical reaction are baking soda and vinegar. When baking soda and vinegar are mixed together, bubbles form! Making a pretend volcano is a classic example of a science experiment that uses baking soda and vinegar. When making a volcano, baking soda and vinegar are added together to create a bunch of bubbles. These bubbles then flow out the top of the volcano and look like lava!

In this experiment, you will be using a similar method to making a pretend volcano, but instead you will be making colourful foaming shapes!

The best part about this experiment is that you can make as many shapes as you want! The experiment can keep going and going, making more and MORE colourful bubbles!

Are you ready to burst some bubbles, junior scientists? Let's dive into this experiment!

Activity 1: Hypothesis

In this experiment, you will be moulding shapes out of baking soda and gelatin. Gelatin can be found in snacks like Jell-O! Based on what you know about baking soda and gelatin, what do you think will happen when the two powders are added together with water?

Use this space to write down your hypothesis.

Experiment Time!

It's that time again, let's collect all of the materials needed for this experiment!

Materials

- Baking soda
- White vinegar
- Gelatin
- Water
- Food colouring
- Large bowl
- Spoons
- Cups
- Large baking tray
- Parchment paper
- Silicone cookie cutters (any shapes you want!)
- Measuring cups (1-cup and ½-cup)
- 1-teaspoon measuring spoon
- 4 eyedroppers
- Paper towel

Now that all of the materials are ready, let's experiment!

 Hey, junior scientists! In the methods section of this experiment, you will be asked to measure multiples of some materials—for example, measuring 2 cups of baking soda using a 1-cup measuring cup. To dwo this, you will need to fill the 1-cup measuring cup twice and add it to the bowl each time it is filled.

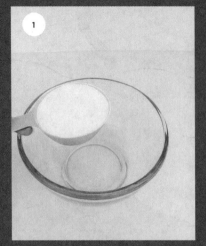

Adding the first cup of baking soda to the mixing bowl using the 1-cup measuring cup.

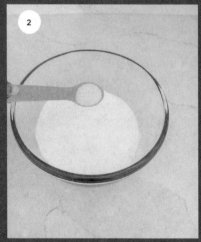

Adding the first teaspoon of gelatin to the mixing bowl using the 1-teaspoon measuring spoon.

Adding water to the mixing bowl using the ½-cup measuring cup.

Mixing all ingredients together using a spoon.

Silicone cookie cutter placed on parchment paper on baking tray.

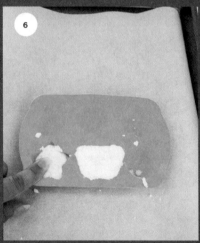

Pressing baking soda/gelatin mixture into cookie cutter mould.

Methods

1. Using the 1-cup measuring cup, measure 2 cups of baking soda and add it to your big mixing bowl.

2. Using the 1-teaspoon measuring spoon, measure 2 teaspoons of gelatin and add it to the same big mixing bowl.

3. Using the ½-cup measuring cup, measure ½ cup of water and add it to the same big mixing bowl.

4. Using a spoon, mix all of the ingredients in the big mixing bowl together.

5. Next, put a piece of parchment paper on the large baking tray. Be sure the parchment paper is covering the entire tray. Place the cookie cutters of your choice on the baking tray.

6. Finally, using your hands, mould the baking soda/gelatin mixture together and press it into the cookie cutters.

7. Once all of the shapes are moulded, place the baking tray in the freezer for one or two hours.

Watch how to make fizzing shapes here!

Activity 2: Observations

Did your hands get dirty while moulding your shapes? Go and wash them off so that you can once again put your artistic skills to the test. It's time to make your first set of observations!

 Use the space to draw what you saw in the mixing bowl after the water was added to the baking soda and gelatin. Did it look soft or hard? What did the mixture look like after moulding it into the cookie cutters?

Experiment Time!

Are you ready to make some colourful bubbles that POP?
The waiting game is over, let's continue the experiment!

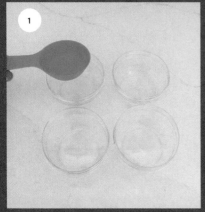

Adding ½ cup of vinegar to each of the four bowls using the ½-cup measuring cup.

Food colouring and eyedroppers added to each of the bowls of vinegar.

Moulded shapes placed on parchment paper on the baking tray.

Adding coloured vinegar to moulded shape.

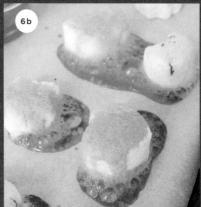

Foaming shapes.

Hey, junior scientist! Did you know that scientists use measuring devices like these eyedroppers in research labs? My mom told me they are called pipettes. She used them to measure accurate amounts of liquids when doing her PhD research! I guess that means we are doing junior PhDs here!

Methods Continued

1. Line up four cups in front of you. Using the ½-cup measuring cup, add ½ cup of vinegar to each cup.

2. Choose four colours of food colouring and add one colour to each of the four cups of vinegar. Mix each with a different spoon.

3. Place an eyedropper in each of the cups with the coloured vinegar.

4. Take the tray with the shapes out of the freezer.

5. Carefully remove each shape from the cookie cutter. Place the cookie cutters to the side so that only the baking soda shapes are left on the parchment paper.

6. Using the droppers, squeeze up the vinegar and squeeze it out onto the shapes. Watch the bubbles form!

Activity 3: Results

How colourful and bubbly do your shapes look?

If you got a little messy during this part of the experiment, take a second to wash up, and get ready to document your results.

Draw a picture of the foaming shapes you made. Be sure to draw what the shapes looked like before and after you added the coloured mixture to the shape. Don't be afraid to get close to the foaming shapes so that you can see all of the tiny bubbles pop!

What's the Science?

This experiment teaches us about acid-base reactions. **Acids** and **bases** are two special types of chemicals. Almost all liquids are either an acid or a base to some degree. The type of ions in a liquid determines if the liquid is an acid or a base. Acids are filled with **hydrogen ions** and bases are filled with **hydroxide ions**. Alternatively, acids release hydrogen ions into a solution and bases absorb them!

Scientists use a device called the **pH scale** to determine how acidic (how much of an acid) or basic (how much of a base) a liquid is. This pH scale is broken down into 14 parts. A liquid that has a pH between 1 and 6 is considered acidic, whereas a liquid that has a pH between 8 and 14 is considered basic. A liquid with a pH of 7 is considered neutral.

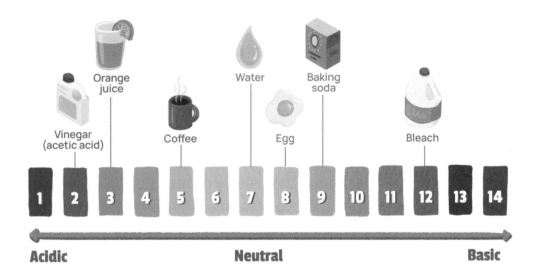

Labelled diagram of a pH scale with examples.

You can find acids and bases all around your house! Liquids that are acidic include orange juice, coffee, and vinegar. Things that are basic include eggs, bleach, and baking soda! But just because two things are both acidic or basic, that doesn't mean they have the same chemical properties. For example, you can eat eggs (because they are only slightly basic), whereas you CANNOT drink bleach (because it is a VERY strong base).

In this experiment, foaming shapes are made by the chemical reaction between two main ingredients: baking soda and vinegar. Baking soda (also known as **sodium bicarbonate**) is a base, and vinegar (also known as **acetic acid**) is an acid. When sodium bicarbonate and acetic acid are mixed together, they undergo a chemical reaction forming carbon dioxide, water, and sodium acetate.

When the coloured vinegar was added to the moulded shapes, a chemical reaction happened, and carbon dioxide gas was formed. Carbon dioxide is a **gas**, and it really wants to escape into the air where other gases are. As a result, the carbon dioxide gas forms tiny bubbles and pops into the air, where it can escape. These are the colourful bubbles that you see!

Talk about a science experiment that really makes your junior scientist skills POP! Well done! Keep what you learned in this experiment in your mind. The next experiment will explore something similar!

Let's Try Again

Uh-oh! Did your shapes not hold their mould? Perhaps they melted too quickly once the vinegar was added?

Let's take a look at how we can modify (or change) the experiment to give us better results.

This is another experiment that usually gives us great results. Chances are, you saw bubbles form when the vinegar was added to your shape. BUT that doesn't mean we can't make the experiment even better! Either way, here is an opportunity for us to try the experiment again.

Modified Methods

1. Add one cup of water to the baking soda mixture instead of ½ cup of water.
2. Put the moulded shapes in the freezer overnight.

Activity 4: Your Turn!

Use the suggestions to plan a new experiment. Complete the new experiment and observe the results you get.

Trial 1

The first modification involves adding 1 cup of water to the baking soda mixture instead of ½ cup of water.

Hypothesis

_____

_____

_____

_____

_____

Modified Methods

_____

_____

_____

_____

_____

Results

Trial 2

The second modification involves putting the moulded shapes in the freezer overnight instead of for only one or two hours.

Hypothesis

Modified Methods

_____

_____

_____

_____

_____

_____

Results

_____

_____

_____

_____

_____

_____

Amazing work, junior scientist! Let's move on to the next experiment.

Bubbles and Balloons

Did you have fun making colourful bubbles in the last experiment? I hope so, because this experiment uses the same type of chemical reaction to blow up balloons!

In this experiment, you will be exploring an acid-base reaction again. But this time, you will use the chemical reaction to help blow up a balloon! Traditionally we blow up balloons using the air in our mouths or air from a machine. The one thing both methods have in common is that they use air (which is a gas) to fill up the space in the balloon.

The air that we breathe out is mostly made up of nitrogen gas and a small amount of carbon dioxide gas. Keep this in mind as we move through the experiment. Another gas that is commonly used to blow up balloons is helium gas. Helium gas is lighter (less dense) than air, meaning it weighs less than air. Because helium gas is so light, it causes balloons to float up in the air when they are filled with it!

In this experiment, we won't use helium gas, but we will use the gas that is produced in the chemical reaction that we will do! You may even have the chance to blow up other things in your house like a balloon!

Who is ready to blow up a balloon with science? I AM! It's time to blow through this experiment, junior scientist!

Activity 1: Hypothesis

In this experiment, you will be using baking soda and vinegar to blow up a balloon. Based on what you learned about the chemical reaction using baking soda and vinegar in the last experiment, how do you think the reaction will help blow up a balloon?

Use this space to write down your hypothesis.

Experiment Time!

This experiment only needs a few simple materials. Let's get them ready now!

Materials

- Baking soda
- White vinegar
- 500 ml empty water bottle
- ½-cup measuring cup
- Funnel
- Spoon
- Balloons
- Paper towel

- Mentos
  (for Let's Try Again section)
- Coke
  (for Let's Try Again section)
- Rubber glove
  (for Let's Try Again section)
- Plastic bag
  (for Let's Try Again section)
- Elastic bands
  (for Let's Try Again section)

Great work preparing all the materials. It's now time to experiment!

Methods

1. Use the ½-cup measuring cup to measure ½ cup of vinegar. Use the funnel to pour the vinegar into the empty water bottle.

2. Next, dry the funnel with a paper towel. Make sure the funnel is completely dry on the inside and outside.

3. Place the dry funnel into the opening of a balloon.

4. Slowly add three spoons of baking soda into the funnel. After each spoon, rub the balloon around in your fingers to help move the baking soda from the funnel into the balloon.

5. In this next step, it is important to keep the baking soda in the bottom of the balloon and not let it fall into the water bottle. Slowly put the opening of the balloon onto the opening of the water bottle. The balloon should be hanging (with the baking soda inside of it) to the side of the bottle.

Watch how to blow up a balloon with science here!

Pouring vinegar into a water bottle using the ½-cup measuring cup.

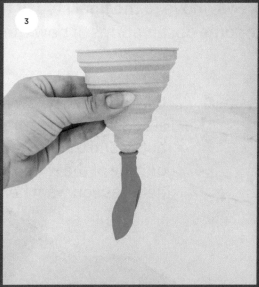

Funnel placed in the opening of the balloon.

Adding baking soda to the balloon using the funnel.

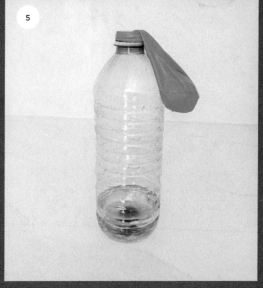

Attaching the balloon to the opening of the water bottle.

Activity 2: Observations

Before we move to the final step of this experiment, take a moment to make some observations of how the experiment is set up.

 Use the space below to draw the water bottle and balloon set up as it is now. Draw what you see inside of the water bottle and the shape of the balloon hanging on the outside of the water bottle. Have fun and add as much detail as you want here.

Experiment Time!

Thank you for waiting so patiently. The time has come to do the final, and most exciting, part of the experiment!

Methods Continued

Lifting the balloon so baking soda can fall into the water bottle.

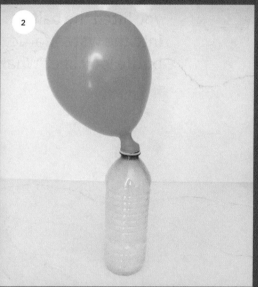

Balloon blowing up.

1. Without taking the balloon off the water bottle, carefully lift the balloon up to allow the baking soda inside the balloon to fall into the water bottle.

2. Step back and watch what happens!

 Hey, junior scientist! If the baking soda is stuck in the balloon and won't come out, try rubbing your finger around the opening of the balloon and water bottle to help the baking soda fall more freely into the water bottle.

Activity 3: Results

And just like that, you blew up a balloon without actually blowing up the balloon! Your lungs must be thanking you. Who would have thought that a chemical reaction could blow up a balloon?!

 Draw a picture of the water bottle and balloon set up after you lifted the balloon and allowed the baking soda to fall into the water bottle. What does the inside of the water bottle look like? What does the balloon look like?

What's the Science?

This experiment is similar to the last experiment because the chemical reaction involved is an acid-base reaction. Remember back to what we learned earlier: vinegar is an acid and baking soda is a base. When vinegar and baking soda are mixed together, carbon dioxide gas is produced.

In this experiment, we created a **closed system** with the water bottle and balloon. A closed system is a special place that *does not* let any solids, liquids, or gases enter or leave it. You can think of this as a small room with all of the windows and doors closed, not allowing anyone or anything to enter or leave.

The opposite of a closed system is an open system. An **open system** is a special place that *does* allow other solids, liquids, or gases to enter and leave it. You can think of this as a small room with all of the windows and doors open, allowing people to enter and leave and allowing wind to flow through.

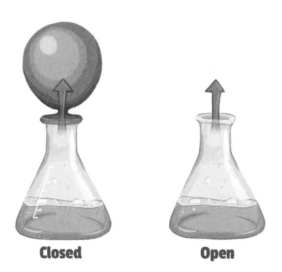

Closed   **Open**

In this experiment, the water bottle and balloon are so tightly joined together, they create a closed system. Now, the carbon dioxide gas created from the chemical reaction between the baking soda and vinegar really wants to escape into the air where other gases are. Since the water bottle is a closed system, the carbon dioxide gas cannot leave. The only option is for the carbon dioxide gas to go up into the balloon, causing it to expand. The flow of carbon dioxide gas from the water bottle up into the balloon is what blows up the balloon, making it bigger and BIGGER!

Let's Try Again

This may be the first experiment so far where nothing went wrong! You are becoming very skilled junior scientists, congratulations! But there will always be opportunities to learn and grow as curious scientists.

 Here are a few ways you can modify this experiment to explore different results. Some of these changes may even make your mind burst with excitement!

Modified Methods

1. Add ½ cup Coke to the water bottle instead of vinegar. Add two Mentos tablets to the balloon instead of baking soda.

2. Use a plastic bag instead of a balloon.

3. Use a plastic glove instead of a balloon.

Activity 4: Your Turn!

Use the suggestions to plan a new experiment. Complete the new experiment and observe the results you get.

Trial 1

The first modification involves adding ½ cup of Coke to the water bottle instead of vinegar. Next, add two Mentos tablets to the balloon instead of baking soda.

Adding Mentos tablet to balloon.

Adding Coke to the water bottle.

Hypothesis

Modified Methods

_____

_____

_____

_____

_____

_____

_____

Results

_____

_____

_____

_____

_____

_____

_____

_____

Trial 2

The second modification involves using a plastic bag instead of a balloon. You can use an elastic band to secure the plastic bag on the water bottle. Everything else in the experiment stays the same.

Plastic bag secured to water bottle.

Hypothesis

_____

_____

_____

_____

_____

_____

Modified Methods

Results

Trial 3

The fourth modification involves using a plastic glove instead of a balloon. You can use an elastic band to secure the plastic glove on the water bottle. Everything else in the experiment stays the same.

Rubber glove attached to the water bottle.

Hypothesis

_____

_____

_____

_____

_____

_____

_____

Modified Methods

Results

 Well done modifying this experiment! You are officially halfway through this book of experiments!

Bouncing Eggs

What's your favourite breakfast food? Mine is eggs, and so is my mom's! I love hard-boiled eggs, scrambled eggs, over-easy eggs, and even BOUNCY eggs. Yes, you heard me correctly—eggs can bounce! Let me show you in this next experiment.

In this experiment, you will be exploring a chemical reaction that will turn a hard-shelled egg into a soft-and-squishy-shelled egg! The end result will be an egg that can bounce like a ball. After you make your giant bouncing egg, you will test out just how high it can bounce by dropping it from different heights. But, keep in mind, it will be very delicate and can burst easily.

This experiment also uses vinegar as its star ingredient. Vinegar is made of a special chemical that reacts with another special chemical in eggshells. This reaction is what causes the shell to disappear! You will learn more about how and why this happens after you do the experiment.

Are you ready to do an EGG-celent experiment? Let's dive in and make a giant bouncing egg!

Activity 1: Hypothesis

In this experiment, you will be using vinegar as the main ingredient to make the bouncing egg. What do you think the vinegar will do to the eggshell? Think back to how vinegar was used in the chemical reactions in experiments 4 and 5.

Use this space to write down your hypothesis.

Experiment Time!

All you need for this experiment are a few simple ingredients. Let's grab them all now.

Materials

- Raw egg (un-cracked)
- White vinegar
- Large mason jar (big enough to fit egg inside)
- Water
- Paper towel
- Ruler or measuring tape
- Baking tray

Are you ready to get your bounce on? Let's go!

Methods

Raw egg in a mason jar filled with vinegar.

Closed mason jar.

Watch how to make a bouncing rubber egg here!

1. Carefully place the raw egg into the large mason jar.

2. Fill the mason jar with vinegar until it covers the entire egg.

3. Screw on the lid of the mason jar. Set the mason jar aside for three days.

Activity 2: Observations

While our bouncing egg is being made, let's take a moment to make some initial observations.

Use the space below to draw what the egg looks like inside of the mason jar. While you draw, consider these questions. What size is the egg? What colour is the egg? What colour is the vinegar?

Experiment Time!

The wait is over. It is now time to bounce this egg!

Methods Continued

Egg after being washed under water.

Setup of how to measure bouncing egg

1. Carefully take the egg out of the mason jar.

2. Turn on the sink tap, allowing water to slowly flow out. Carefully rub the outside of the egg under the stream of water to get all the small pieces of shell off.

It is important to be very gentle here. The bouncing egg is delicate and can burst easily if you squeeze it.

3. Place the bouncing egg on the baking tray.

4. Stand the ruler up and make note of where the marks are for 5 cm, 10 cm, 20 cm, and 30 cm.

5. Hold the egg up at 5 cm above the baking tray and drop it. What happened? Write it in the chart in the results section on the next page.

6. Repeat step 5 by dropping the egg from 10 cm, 20 cm, and 30 cm. Write down what happens after each drop in the chart in the results section next.

Activity 3: Results

How high did your egg bounce? Did it go SPLAT after one of the drops?

 Draw a picture of the bouncing egg. Take out a fresh egg and compare the two eggs. Has the size of the egg changed after being placed in the vinegar for three days? Has the colour of the egg changed?

Height	Observation	Did the egg break (Yes or No)?
5 cm		
10 cm		
20 cm		
30 cm		

What's the Science?

In this experiment, a chemical reaction happened to make your bouncing egg. The star of the chemical reaction was the vinegar added to your raw egg. The vinegar reacted with the eggshell to make it disappear!

Eggshells are made of a substance called **calcium carbonate**. If you remember back to the last experiment, vinegar reacted with baking soda to create a bunch of tiny bubbles of carbon dioxide gas. The calcium carbonate in the eggshell reacted with the vinegar in this experiment in the same way that the baking soda (which is sodium hydrogen carbonate—do you see the connection?) reacted with vinegar in the last two experiments. When vinegar (a weak acid) is added to calcium carbonate in the eggshell (a base), a chemical reaction happens, forming carbon dioxide gas and calcium ions. This is why you may have noticed that there were a bunch of tiny bubbles on the eggshell as it sat in the vinegar for a few days.

Once the entire eggshell is dissolved by the vinegar, all that is left behind is a thin membrane protecting the egg. A **membrane** is a thin substance that protects things from an outside environment. Here, the membrane keeps the egg whites and yolk inside the egg and only allows certain things from the outside to enter.

The membrane of a chicken egg is selectively permeable. **Selectively permeable** membranes only allow certain things to enter and leave them (you can think of them as a gate opening or closing only for certain cars). Vinegar is one of the substances that is allowed to enter the egg's membrane.

Once the eggshell is completely gone, the vinegar passes through the membrane of the egg and into the egg through a process called osmosis. **Osmosis** is the movement of water across a semipermeable membrane. Water likes to move from an area where there is a lot of water to an area where there is a small amount of water. In this experiment, there is more water in the vinegar than there is inside the egg. As a result, the vinegar (and water) passes through the semipermeable egg membrane and moves from the jar into the inside of the egg. That is why the egg looks bigger after sitting in the vinegar for a few days.

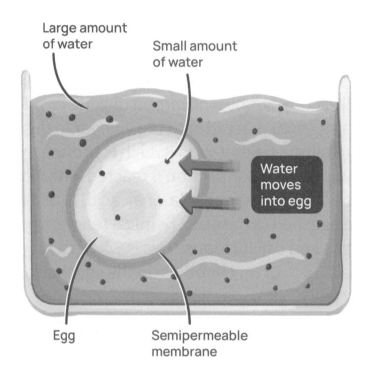

Illustration of the egg's selectively permeable membrane and osmosis happening.

If you want to shrink the egg again, you can place it in an environment that doesn't have water in it. This will make the vinegar (and water) inside the egg move through the semipermeable membrane and leave the egg. You will have a chance to try this in the next section!

Let's Try Again

Oh no! Something went wrong! Your egg didn't lose all of its shell. Below is a suggestion for how you can remove all of the egg's shell.

 Hey junior scientist! Did you notice the egg got bigger after sitting in vinegar for three days? Well, there is a way we can shrink it back down to a smaller size! One of the modified methods that you will do next will help shrink the egg.

Modified Methods

1. Leave the egg sitting in the vinegar for five days.
2. After the experiment is completed, place the egg in a bowl of salt for three days.

Activity 4: Your Turn!

Use the suggestions to plan a new experiment. Complete the new experiment and observe the results you get.

Trial 1

The first modification involves letting the egg sit in the vinegar for five days. Don't forget to put the lid on the jar so that the vinegar doesn't evaporate!

Hypothesis

_____

_____

_____

_____

_____

Modified Methods

_____

_____

_____

_____

_____

_____

_____

_____

_____

_____

_____

Trial 2

The second modification involves putting the bouncing egg in a bowl of salt for three days. This can only be completed after you do the first part of the experiment and make the bouncing egg.

Hypothesis

_____

_____

_____

_____

_____

_____

_____

Modified Methods

Results

Watch how to shrink a bouncing egg!

Well done! You just reversed one of the results of this experiment! I hope this didn't make you hungry. If it did, take a little break now and go get a snack. Food will fuel your brain for the remainder of these experiments. BUT remember to clean up first—we never want to eat while doing science experiments.

Invisible Ink

Have you ever wanted to be a detective and uncover secret messages? I have! That's why I love this next science experiment. I am going to teach you how to make special secret messages that you can send to your friends and family!

In this experiment, you will be exploring a chemical reaction that will make secret messages appear on paper. The star of this experiment will be the invisible ink that you make!

The star of this experiment is the juice from a citrus fruit. Citrus fruits include oranges, lemons, limes, pomelos, grapefruits, and so many more! This juice will help us make invisible ink!

Believe it or not, this method was used by George Washington's army to send secret messages during the American Revolutionary War, almost three hundred years ago. This is the stamp in history that made America the independent country it is today! Imagine how many citrus fruits they needed to use to send all those messages!

Are you ready to do a top-secret experiment? Let's make some invisible ink, junior scientists!

Activity 1: Hypothesis

In this experiment, you will be using the juice from a citrus fruit to make invisible ink. What do you think the citrus fruit has in it that will help this science experiment happen? Hint: A lot of people like citrus fruits because they are SWEET!

Use this space
to write down
your hypothesis.

Experiment Time!

It is time to collect all the materials you need for this experiment.

Materials

- Whole lemon (or lemon juice)
- Cotton swabs
- White printer paper
- Small bowl

- Candle (or incandescent light bulb, or electric stove element set to low)
- Matches (or incandescent light bulb or electric stove element set to low)

 Hey, junior scientists! You will be using a heat source in this experiment. Please have an adult work with you when it's time to use the candle, light bulb, or electric stove element (step 5). Safety first!

Put on your investigator hat and coat. Let's write some secret messages!

Methods

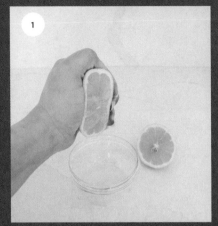

Squeezing lemon juice into the bowl.

Dipping a cotton swab into the lemon juice.

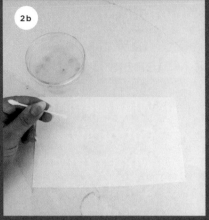

Writing a secret message with lemon juice using the cotton swab.

1. Squeeze the juice of one lemon into the small bowl. If you are using a whole lemon, ask an adult to cut it in half for you. If you are using lemon juice from a bottle, pour a small amount into the small bowl.

2. Take a cotton swab and dip it into the lemon juice.

3. Using the wet cotton swab, write a message on the white printer paper. You can write any secret message you wish!

4. Leave the paper to dry for at least 10 minutes.

Watch how to make secret messages here!

Activity 2: Observations

While your paper is drying, take some time to make your first set of observations.

 Use the space below to draw what the piece of paper looks like before it begins to dry, and after it dries completely. What colour is the paper? What colour is the lemon juice?

Experiment Time!

Your paper is dry! It's time to uncover your secret messages!

Methods Continued

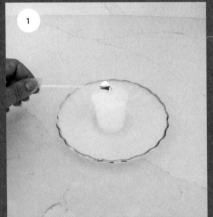
Lighting a candle with a match.

Holding a dried piece of paper over the candle flame.

Secret message appearing.

1. Ask an adult to help you light the candle with a match. Or, if you are using an incandescent light bulb, ask the adult to help turn on the light bulb for you. Or, if you are using an electric stove element (on low), ask an adult to assist you.

2. Place the paper with your secret message on it one inch over the heat source (candle flame or light bulb).

3. Watch your secret message slowly appear!

Activity 3: Results

Do you feel like a top-secret agent yet? Take this time to write out and draw your final results.

 Draw a picture of the paper with your secret message on it. What colour is the paper? What colour is the "invisible ink"? Think about how the colour of the ink changed before and after it was placed over the heat source.

What's the Science?

In this experiment, a chemical reaction happened to make invisible ink appear! The star of this chemical reaction is the lemon juice that you used to write the secret messages.

Lemon juice, and many other fruit juices, contain sugar. Sugar is made up of **carbon atoms**. Carbon compounds (sugars in the fruit) are colourless at room temperature, which means you cannot see them. When exposed to heat, carbon compounds are broken down into individual carbon atoms.

When carbon atoms are exposed to air, they go through a process called oxidation. **Oxidation** is a chemical reaction where a substance loses electrons. When an oxidation reaction happens in air, the carbon atoms gain oxygen. When this happens, the properties of the substance change, causing the substance to turn from light to dark in colour.

An example of where you see oxidation reactions happen in your kitchen is when you cut an apple and leave it out on a plate. You notice that the apple begins to change to a brown colour. This happens because the sugars in the apple go through an oxidation chemical reaction with the air.

In this experiment, the heat (from the candle flame or light bulb) causes the sugars (carbon compounds) in the lemon juice to break down into individual carbon atoms. The carbon atoms are then exposed to air and an oxidation reaction happens. This changes the lemon juice from colourless to brown, revealing your secret message!

Let's Try Again

Oh no! Something went wrong! Your message didn't appear!

 Don't worry, junior scientist, we are all in this together. Remember, failure is normal. It teaches us lessons that make us better, smarter, and stronger in the end. Let's work through this little bump in the road and modify the experiment together.

Modified Methods

1. After the lemon juice dries on the paper, trace your writing to add one more layer of juice.

Activity 4: Your Turn!

Use the suggestion to plan a new experiment. Complete the new experiment and observe the results you get.

Trial 1

This modification involves adding two layers of invisible ink (lemon juice) to write your message. After the first layer of juice dries, add a second layer.

Hypothesis

Modified Methods

Results

Experiment 8

Penny Chemistry

Have you ever found a penny lying around your house, or perhaps on the sidewalk outside, and noticed it was dirty in colour? Perhaps instead of being a shiny copper coin, it was a dull and dark bluish-green coin. This happens because, over time, the copper of the penny reacts with oxygen in the air to form a new substance (that isn't as shiny and bright as copper)!

Two large-scale examples are the peak of the Peace Tower of Canada's Parliament Building, and the Statue of Liberty in the United States of America! The Statue of Liberty is known for its beautiful bright blue-green colour. But did you know that it hasn't always been that colour? The statue is covered in copper plates, and so the original colour of the statue was copper. Over time, as the copper reacted with oxygen in the air, the colour of the statue turned from a shiny copper to a bluish-green tint.

In this experiment, you will be exploring a chemical reaction in a way that involves using pennies! Don't worry, you won't be wasting any money here, you will be cleaning it! The star of this next science experiment is a penny! Here, you will learn how to make a penny bright and shiny again. You will also learn how to quickly make the penny dirty again!

 The star of this chemical reaction is the copper in the penny. Unfortunately, pennies made after 1982 are made of two metals: copper and zinc. But pennies made before 1982 are made of solid copper! That means, if you are able to find some pennies from before 1982, the experiment will be even better!

Are you ready to dive into an experiment that really makes CENTS? Let's go!

Activity 1: Hypothesis

In this experiment, you will be using vinegar and salt to help clean the dirty pennies. Based on what you have learned about vinegar in previous experiments in this book, what property do you think it has that will help clean the pennies?

Use this space to write down your hypothesis.

Experiment Time!

It's that time again—let's collect all the materials involved in this experiment. You won't have to travel far, because everything can be found in your kitchen!

Materials

- 6 dull pennies
- Vinegar
- Water
- Salt
- 1-teaspoon measuring spoon
- 1-tablespoon measuring spoon
- 3 small bowls
- 3 pieces of printer paper
- Salt
- Paper towel

Great work collecting everything for this experiment. Let's put on our lab coats and get to work!

Methods

Watch how to clean your pennies here!

1. Place a piece of white paper in front of you. Write the following three labels:
   - Water
   - Water + vinegar
   - Water + vinegar + salt

2. Place three bowls on the sheet of paper and add two dull pennies to each bowl.

Setup of dull pennies in each of the three bowls.

Activity 2: Observations

Before you add any liquid to the bowl, take some time to observe what the pennies look like right now.

 Use the space below to draw what the pennies looks like before you clean them. What colour are they? Can you read what is written on them? Be sure to make six separate drawings, one for each of the six pennies. Use the chart below to organize your observations.

	Penny 1	Penny 2
Bowl 1		
Bowl 2		
Bowl 3		

Experiment Time!

Now for the fun part. It is time to clean our pennies with science!

Methods Continued

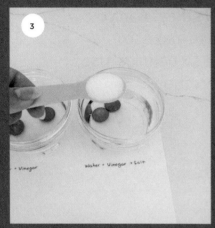
Adding water to bowl with vinegar and water.

Pennies sitting in each of their experiment bowls for five minutes.

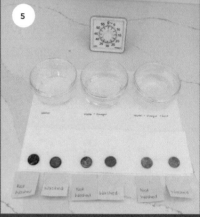
Setup of pennies after they have been removed from their bowls and either washed or not.

1. Add 1 tablespoon of water to the first bowl, labelled "water."

2. Fill the second bowl, labelled "water + vinegar," with vinegar, just enough to cover the penny. Add 1 tablespoon of water to the bowl.

3. Add 1 teaspoon of salt to the third bowl, labelled "water + vinegar + salt," and fill the bowl with vinegar, just enough to cover the penny. Add 1 tablespoon of water to the bowl.

4. Leave the pennies in the bowls for five minutes. Watch what happens over time.

5. After five minutes, take the pennies out of the bowls. Place one penny from each bowl on a piece of paper towel in front of the bowls' labels. Take the other pennies, rinse them under water, and place them on their respective paper towels. Write labels on your paper towels so you will know which towel has the rinsed pennies.

6. Make observations of the pennies after one minute, ten minutes, and one hour.

Activity 3: Results

After the pennies are dry, it is time to collect your final results.

Write out and draw what each penny looks like after sitting in their different bowls. Write separate results for each of the six pennies using the chart below. Has the colour of the penny changed? Can you read what is written on each penny?

	Penny 1 (washed)	Penny 2 (unwashed)
Bowl 1	1 min: 10 min: 1 hour:	1 min: 10 min: 1 hour:
Bowl 2	1 min: 10 min: 1 hour:	1 min: 10 min: 1 hour:
Bowl 3	1 min: 10 min: 1 hour:	1 min: 10 min: 1 hour:

What's the Science?

In this experiment, a chemical reaction happened to help clean your pennies! Pennies are coins that are coated with copper. **Copper** is a soft and shiny metal that gives pennies their reddish-orange colour. Over time, when copper is exposed to oxygen in the air, it goes through an **oxidation reaction** and forms copper oxide. **Copper oxide** is responsible for the dark "dirty" spots you see on old pennies.

The stars of this chemical reaction are vinegar and salt. Vinegar contains an **acid** known as acetic acid. Salt, also known as sodium chloride, reacts with the vinegar to produce a very weak solution of hydrogen chloride. This new acid removes the copper oxide from the pennies, replacing it with copper chloride, which brings back their shiny copper colour!

When the pennies are taken out of the vinegar solutions and rinsed under water, the chemical reaction stops. Over time, those pennies will react with oxygen in the air to form copper oxide and become dull in colour again. However, this reaction is slow, meaning you won't be able to see it here.

However, the un-rinsed pennies still have some vinegar on them. Vinegar acts to speed up the oxidation process on the penny. Over the course of a few hours, the pennies that were in the vinegar (and not rinsed under water) react with oxygen in the air to form bluish-green copper oxide again. That is why you saw a bluish-green substance on those pennies that were not washed.

Now, what about the pennies placed in water? You may have noticed nothing happened to pennies placed in only water. In this experiment, we used water as the experiment control. An **experiment control** is an element in an experiment that is not changed. Scientists use experiment controls in all of their experiments to confirm and compare the results collected.

Talk about a science experiment that really makes cents!

Let's Try Again

Oh no! Something went wrong! Your penny didn't get shiny!

 It's time to put our skills to the test as junior scientists and change this experiment. You are becoming a pro at changing experiments and trying new things! What do you think we can do here to make the experiment work better?

Modified Methods

1. Leave the pennies in their third bowls for ten minutes.
2. Add 2 teaspoons of salt to the third bowl instead of 1 teaspoon.

Activity 4: Your Turn!

Use the suggestions to plan a new experiment. Complete the new experiment and observe the results you get.

Trial 1

The first modification involves leaving the pennies in their bowls for ten minutes to allow the reaction to run for longer.

Hypothesis

_____

_____

_____

_____

_____

Modified methods

_____

_____

_____

_____

_____

_____

_____

_____

_____

_____

_____

Trial 2

The second modification involves adding 2 teaspoons of salt to the third bowl of vinegar instead of 1 teaspoon.

Hypothesis

_____

_____

_____

_____

_____

_____

_____

Modified methods

Results

Well done, junior scientists! Do you see how all of the science experiments are slowly coming together?

Bending Bones

 My mom always tells me to drink my milk to help keep my bones strong! She told me it's because milk has calcium in it! This next science experiment will explore the calcium in bones!

Calcium is a mineral that is needed to make healthy bones. In fact, 99 percent of the calcium in our bodies is stored in bones! But our bodies can't make calcium on their own, so we need to get calcium from our diet. Calcium is found in foods like cheese, milk, leafy greens like spinach, yogurt, and best of all, ICE CREAM!

As people age, the amount of calcium in their bones decreases. This means their bones get weak, soft, and brittle. That's why doctors suggest that people take calcium supplements as they get older, to help keep their bones strong.

In this experiment, you will explore a way to remove the calcium from bones. The end result will be a magic bone that isn't hard anymore! A chemical reaction will be used to make your magic bones, and the star of the chemical reaction will yet again be vinegar!

Are you ready to do a bone-breaking experiment!! Let's get started!

Activity 1: Hypothesis

In this experiment, you will be using vinegar once again to change the strength and hardness of a bone. Based on what you have learned about vinegar and calcium substances in past experiments, what do you think will happen in this experiment?

Use this space to write down your hypothesis.

Experiment Time!

Are you ready to gather the materials for this experiment?
Ready. Set. GO!

Materials

- 1 clean and dry chicken bone (drumsticks work best)
- White vinegar
- Glass jar with lid
- Scissors
- Paper towel

Hey, junior scientists! The best way to get a chicken bone is to keep a bone after you have chicken for dinner one night. If you don't eat chicken, you can purchase a cooked piece of chicken (drumsticks work best) from a local grocery store, remove all the meat from it, and set it on the counter to dry for an hour.

Methods

Watch how to make a rubber bone here

Dry chicken bone placed in empty mason jar.

1. Take the dry chicken bone and place it in the glass jar.

Activity 2: Observations

Before you add anything to the jar with the bone in it, take a moment to write down your initial observations of the bone.

 Use the space below to draw what the bone looks like. Also describe how the bone feels. Is the bone hard? Is the bone soft? Can you bend the bone in half? Make note of any special features you notice about the bone.

Experiment Time!

The time has come—let's make a magic bone!

Methods Continued

Setup of chicken bone in vinegar in closed mason jar.

1. Fill the glass jar with vinegar until the bone is completely covered in liquid.

2. Screw on the lid of the jar.

3. Place the jar on the counter for four days.

4. After four days have passed, take the bone out of the vinegar, and dry it with paper towel.

Activity 3: Results

Now that the bone is dry, it's time to document the final results.

Write out and draw what the bone looks like after sitting in the vinegar for four days. Describe how the bone feels. Is the bone hard? Is the bone soft? Can you bend the bone in half?

After you write down your final observations, take a pair of scissors and try to cut the bone in half. Draw what the inside of the bone looks like.

What's the Science?

In this experiment, a chemical reaction happened to transform a hard bone into a magic soft bone! As we learned earlier, bones are made of bone calcium (in the form of calcium carbonate), bone cells, and collagen. **Collagen** is a soft protein (material) found in bones, skin, and connective tissue (the stuff that holds things together in our bodies).

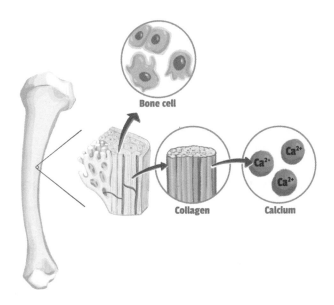

Three main components of bones.

All bones are made of the same materials. That means the bones in our bodies (human bones) are made of the same stuff as chicken bones (used in this experiment). This is why this is a great experiment to show the effect of calcium loss in bones.

The star of this chemical reaction is vinegar. Vinegar was the only substance added to the bone to make it into a magic soft bone. Vinegar contains an acid known as acetic acid. When vinegar meets the calcium carbonate in the chicken bone, substances called calcium acetate and carbonic acid are formed. **Calcium acetate** is a type of salt that dissolves in water (just like table salt dissolves in water).

Carbonic acid is very unstable, which means that it does not want to exist as carbonic acid. As a result, the carbonic acid quickly breaks down into water and carbon dioxide gas. This is why you may have noticed tiny bubbles forming on the chicken bone as it sat in vinegar over the four days.

The result of this multi-step chemical reaction is calcium being removed from the bones. Once the calcium is removed, there are only two materials remaining, bone cells and collagen. Since collagen is a soft and gel-like material, the bone also feels soft and can be bent in half.

There you have it, a science experiment that teaches us the importance of calcium in our diet!

Let's Try Again

Oh no! Something went wrong! Your bone didn't get soft!

 Don't worry, junior scientist, mistakes happen all the time in science labs. There are many possible reasons why the bone didn't get soft and bendy. One of the most common reasons is the size of the bone. Remember what we learned about surface area in Experiment 2. One of these tips explores surface area.

Modified Methods

1. Place the bone in a bigger glass jar than originally used, and fill the jar fully with vinegar.
2. Leave the bone in vinegar for six days.

Activity 4: Your Turn!

Use the suggestions to plan a new experiment. Complete the new experiment and observe the results you get.

Trial 1

The first modification involves placing the bone in a bigger glass jar and filling the jar completely with vinegar.

Hypothesis

_____

_____

_____

_____

Modified methods

_____

_____

_____

_____

_____

_____

_____

_____

_____

_____

_____

_____

Trial 2

The second modification involves leaving the bone in the vinegar for six days.

Hypothesis

_____

_____

_____

_____

_____

_____

Modified methods

Results

Experiment 10

Mini Rockets

Did you know that, back when my mom was a kid, they printed pictures from something called film? Apparently, my grandparents had to buy film in a film canister and put it into a camera just to take pictures! Talk about a lot of work!

Film canisters are going to be the star of this next science experiment. In fact, you are going to use film canisters to build mini rockets! These rockets will be filled by a chemical reaction that will help them blast off into the sky!

The outside of a traditional NASA space rocket is made of a lightweight material like titanium or aluminum. The frame of a space rocket is similar to the frame of an airplane. In this experiment, you will be using film canisters to mimic the outside of a rocket.

The inside of a traditional space rocket is the propulsion system. The **propulsion system** is the part that helps the rocket blast off into space! There are two types of propulsion systems: liquid rocket engines, and solid rocket engines. In a liquid rocket engine, fuel is mixed with an oxidizer and burned to create gas at a high temperature and pressure. This is what pushes the rocket up into space! In this experiment, you will explore a chemical reaction in the film canister to help the rocket blast off into the sky.

Who is ready to do a science experiment that will be mind-BLASTING? Let's take off and begin!

Activity 1: Hypothesis

In this experiment, you will be placing an Alka-Seltzer tablet and water into the film canister to help make your mini rocket. What do you think will happen in the film canister to cause the rocket to pop up into the sky?

Use this space to write down your hypothesis.

Experiment Time!

By now, you know the drill! It's time to collect all the materials needed for this experiment.

Materials

- 1 film canister with lid
- Water
- Alka-Seltzer tablet
- 1-teaspoon measuring spoon
- Paper towel

- Safety goggles (splash goggles or swim goggles)
- Construction paper (for Let's Try Again section)
- Scissors (for Let's Try Again section)

Well done, junior scientists! It's time to start our last experiment.

Methods

Watch how to make a mini rocket here!

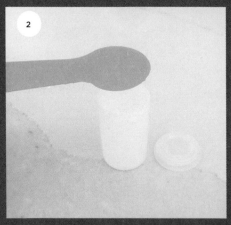

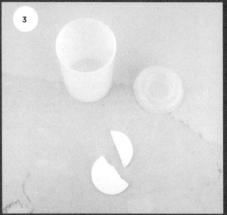

Adding water to film canister using 1-teaspoon measuring spoon. Alka-Seltzer tablet broken in half.

1. Start by putting your safety goggles on. Next, open the film canister.

2. Using the 1-teaspoon measuring spoon, add 1 teaspoon of water to the film canister.

3. Take one Alka-Seltzer tablet and break it in half.

Activity 2: Observations

Before you add the Alka-Seltzer tablet to the film canister, first make an observation of what they both look like.

Use the space below to draw what the Alka-Seltzer tablet looks like. How big is the tablet? What does the tablet feel like? What does the inside of the film canister look like?

Experiment Time!

The time has come! Let's blast off, junior scientists!

Methods Continued

 **CAUTION!** Remember, it's always important to practice safety in a science lab. This experiment is going to POP, so please make sure you do the next part of the methods in an open area. Also make sure you step back right away, so the film canister rocket doesn't hit you.

Closed film canister placed upside down on table.

1. Put the two pieces of the Alka-Seltzer tablets into the film canister and quickly put on the lid. Place the canister upside down.

2. Step back and watch.

 The best part about this experiment is you can do it over and over again! You can even try making multiple rockets at one time. Start with two at one time, and then three, and then four, and so on. See how many rockets you can get to blast off at the same time.

Activity 3: Results

Amazing work! That was so explosive!

 Write out and draw what the mini rocket looked like as it blasted off into the sky. Take a look at the inside of the film canister, what does it look like? What does the Alka-Seltzer tablet look like now? What does the Alka-Seltzer tablet feel like?

What's the Science?

In this experiment, a chemical reaction happened to make your mini rocket blast off into the sky. This science experiment is all about pressure. **Pressure** is the force of all the gas particles divided by the area of the wall surrounding them. For example, the pressure of sand collecting in a bucket would be the weight of the sand divided by the area (or size of the surface) of the bucket.

In chemistry, pressure is usually used to describe gases. In this experiment, pressure builds up inside the rocket to help it blast off into the sky. When the Alka-Seltzer tablet was added to the water in the film canister, a chemical reaction occurred. The product of this chemical reaction was carbon dioxide gas.

If you remember back to previous experiments, you will remember that carbon dioxide gas wants to escape into the air where other gases are. However, in this experiment, the carbon dioxide gas gets trapped in the film canister (similar to the carbon dioxide in the balloon experiment) because the lid is tightly placed on top of the canister. As a result, the carbon dioxide gas cannot leave the canister. The build-up of carbon dioxide gas inside the film canister creates a lot of pressure.

As more carbon dioxide gas is made, more and more pressure builds up. After some time, the build-up of pressure is too much, and so the lid pops off the film canister to help release the carbon dioxide into the air. Because the film canister was upside down on the table, the lid pushed off the surface of the table, causing your mini rocket to blast off into the sky!

Talk about a science experiment that really POPS off!

Let's Try Again

Oh no! Something went wrong! Your mini rocket didn't blast off!

 Well, that was boring, nothing happened! Don't worry, there are many reasons this could have happened. Let's explore some ways we can change this experiment to help your rocket blast off into the sky!

Modified Methods

1. Place two Alka-Seltzer tablets into the film canister instead of one.

2. Be quicker with turning the film canister upside down.

3. Use construction paper to cut out wings that you can then stick onto the sides of the film canister to make a rocket.

Activity 4: Your Turn!

Use the suggestions to plan a new experiment. Complete the new experiment and observe the results you get.

Trial 1

The first modification involves using two Alka-Seltzer tablets instead of one. Break each tablet in half and place all four pieces in the film canister.

Hypothesis

_____

_____

_____

_____

Modified methods

_____

_____

_____

_____

_____

_____

_____

_____

_____

Trial 2

The second modification involves using your speed skills and placing the film canister upside down faster.

Hypothesis

_____

_____

_____

_____

_____

_____

_____

_____

Modified methods

Results

Trial 3

The third modification involves making wings for the rocket out of construction paper.

Rocket ship film canister.

Hypothesis

Modified methods

_____

_____

_____

_____

_____

_____

Results

_____

_____

_____

_____

_____

That's a wrap! Amazing job! Your skills as a junior scientist have improved so much since you first started doing these experiments!

Ingredients Used in Experiments

One of the highlights of this STEAM experiment book is that many of the ingredients (chemicals) used can be found in your house. Below is the complete list of chemicals used in this book.

- Vinegar
- Salt
- Baking soda
- Lemon juice
- Dish soap
- Hydrogen peroxide
- Vegetable oil
- Alka-Seltzer tablets
- Contact lens solution
- Liquid glue
- Gelatin powder
- Coke
- Mentos
- Water

Unit Conversions

Cups	Fluid Ounces (Oz)	Tablespoon (Tbsp)	Teaspoon (Tsp)	Mililiters (ml)
1 cup	8 oz	16 Tbsp	48 Tsp	237 ml
1/2 cup	4 oz	8 Tbsp	24 Tsp	118 ml
1/4 cup	2 oz	4 Tbsp	12 Tsp	59 ml

Measurment	Mililiters (ml)
1 tablespoon (Tbsp)	15 ml
1 teaspoon (Tsp)	5 ml

About the Author

Dr. Sarah Habibi is a molecular biologist, educator, and digital content creator. As a graduate of both doctoral studies and education studies (specific focus STEAM education), Sarah has become an expert at communicating science to audiences of all ages, with a specific focus on children.

The work Sarah has done with making science accessible online has been featured in a publication in the high-impact research journal, PLOS ONE; through media appearances on popular TV broadcasts like Breakfast Television; and through interviews with news outlets like the Toronto Star and Shondaland. Sarah is also an Award-Winning public speaker. The winner of the Three-Minute Thesis competition, she delivered a talk about her PhD research in a compelling and engaging way to an audience of non-experts.

Since then, Sarah has been hired to give talks to high school and university students on topics related to women in STEAM, Science literacy online, and the work she does on TikTok with making science experiments fun. Sarah has also worked with organizations like ComSciCon and Humber College to host virtual workshops on how to effectively communicate science on social media and the importance of learning science through hands-on experimentation.

Most recently, Sarah has worked with some of the biggest brands in North America, like Procter and Gamble, as the Spokesperson for the launch of a new Vicks product in Canada, as well as social media giants like TikTok to deliver professional development workshops geared to teaching at-home science experiments to client partners. As a result, Sarah is committed to sharing her love for science with people of all ages and showcasing the power of social media as a tool for advancing science education for the next generation.

Mango Publishing, established in 2014, publishes an eclectic list of books by diverse authors—both new and established voices—on topics ranging from business, personal growth, women's empowerment, LGBTQ+ studies, health, and spirituality to history, popular culture, time management, decluttering, lifestyle, mental wellness, aging, and sustainable living. We were recently named 2019 *and* 2020's #1 fastest-growing independent publisher by *Publishers Weekly.* Our success is driven by our main goal, which is to publish high-quality books that will entertain readers as well as make a positive difference in their lives.

Our readers are our most important resource; we value your input, suggestions, and ideas. We'd love to hear from you—after all, we are publishing books for you!

Please stay in touch with us and follow us at:

Facebook: Mango Publishing
Twitter: @MangoPublishing
Instagram: @MangoPublishing
LinkedIn: Mango Publishing
Pinterest: Mango Publishing
Newsletter: mangopublishinggroup.com/newsletter

Join us on Mango's journey to reinvent publishing, one book at a time.